The Wesley Challenge
21 Days to a More Authentic Faith
Youth Study Book

The Wesley Challenge:
21 Days to a More Authentic Faith

The Wesley Challenge

978-1-5018-3290-1
978-1-5018-3291-8 eBook

The Wesley Challenge: DVD

978-1-5018-3294-9

The Wesley Challenge: Leader Guide

978-1-5018-3292-5
978-1-5018-3293-2 eBook

The Wesley Challenge: Youth Study Book

978-1-5018-3298-7
978-1-5018-3299-4 eBook

The Wesley Challenge: Campaign Download Package

978-1-5018-3300-7

CHRIS FOLMSBEE

21 DAYS TO A MORE AUTHENTIC FAITH

Adapted for youth by
Lori Jones

Abingdon Press / Nashville

The Wesley Challenge
21 Days to a More Authentic Faith
Youth Study Book

Copyright © 2017 Abingdon Press
All rights reserved.

This book is printed on elemental chlorine-free paper.

978-1-5018-3298-7

17 18 19 20 21 22 23 24 25 — 10 9 8 7 6 5 4 3 2 1
MANUFACTURED IN THE UNITED STATES OF AMERICA

CONTENTS

INTRODUCTION

My teenage son is an expert at video games. He didn't get to be an expert by playing one game, one time, if you know what I mean. No, he plays *a lot*. In order to master a craft or skill, we must do three things—practice, practice, and practice—and we must be disciplined to do it regularly because we only get better at something when we put in the practice time. For instance, we won't be able to do the hard math if we don't first master multiplication tables. We can't make the winning basket if we haven't been doing our free-throw drills. We can't perform our part in the school play if we haven't first memorized our lines.

Over the years, I've spent a lot of time trying to develop certain practices—or habits—that help me grow in my relationship with God, my relationship with myself, and my relationship with others. I've learned that whatever it is I'm practicing—whether prayer, quiet time, reading my Bible—I have to make the time, again and again, in order to make it a habit and a way of life. Simply put, I can't just talk about doing these things—I have to actually *do it*.

This short book is intended to help you do just that—to help you practice the spiritual habits, practices, and actions that can lead you toward a vibrant Christian life. For the next twenty-one days, I'm asking you to explore and consider the twenty-one questions that John and Charles Wesley asked their fellow believers nearly three hundred years ago and to discover how these questions apply to your own life as well.

The 21-Day Challenge

This 21-day challenge is about opening your mind, your heart, and your hands to develop a lifestyle of practicing the disciplines of our Christian faith. The point of these practices is not to make you appear super holy, but to be Jesus' hands and feet in our world. Research shows that it takes twenty-one days to develop a habit, so after sticking with this for three weeks, my hope is that you will have formed a deeper relationship with God and will continue on your life's journey to get to know God more and more.

Over the next twenty-one days, we'll take Wesley's twenty-one questions and ask you to reflect on some meanings behind the questions. Though you can certainly read this book on your own, I hope you'll choose to participate in this 21-day challenge with a group, or with some friends, for I am convinced that discipleship happens best in community.

To the Leader

This book can be read by an individual as a daily devotional, and it can also be used in a group setting. Each week consists of seven daily devotionals, followed by these sections, which can be used in group settings.

Going Deeper

Here you'll find more devotional thoughts and Scriptures that complement the main text for the chapter. This section also includes some reflection thoughts and questions around the week's theme. If you've completed the devotions during the week, it might be helpful to look over this section right before you go to meet with your group.

Sharing Thoughts and Feelings

These group questions can serve as an icebreaker to open your group time together. They will also allow anyone who hasn't read the daily devotionals to be drawn into the conversation.

Doing Things Together

Each weekly session concludes with two fifteen-minute activities designed to engage your group. Supplies are minimal, but be sure that someone is in charge of bringing what you'll need for the activities. Most of the activities wrap up with one or two additional discussion questions or a look back at the text.

Listening for God

To end your session, a prayer is included. You and the group members can use the prayer as is or substitute a prayer of your own.

Week 1

RELATIONSHIP WITH GOD: AN UPWARD FOCUS

"*I am the Vine, you are the branches. When you're joined with me and I with you, the relation intimate and organic, the harvest is sure to be abundant. Separated, you can't produce a thing.*"

John 15:5-8 MSG

Week 1

RELATIONSHIP WITH GOD: AN UPWARD FOCUS

If someone were to ask you, "What's a relationship with God like?" what would you say? How would you respond?

For many of us, the idea of "having a relationship" with God may feel weird or strange, like something that can't really be done. I mean, God's up there, and we're down here, and how exactly are we supposed to know who God is and what God wants? And how is that relationship supposed to affect our lives anyway?

The good news is this: A relationship with God is available to everyone who believes in God, and God even gives us tools for growing in that relationship. Christian practices—such as prayer, Bible reading, and Bible study—shape us and bring us closer to knowing the heart of God. But it's important to note that living out Christian practices is not what saves us or leads us to holiness. Praying or reading a Bible just so you can check it off your Christian to-do list is not what Wesley (or Jesus, for that matter) had in mind. Instead, through a commitment to these practices, our eyes are turned upward to God, and we are able to come alongside God's mission in the world and reflect God's radiant and extravagant love to others.

In the seven questions you will think about over the next few days, Wesley set forth a challenge to become who God created you to be. This week you will be challenged to read, think, reflect, pray, and live out actions that reveal what it means to turn your focus upward, toward God. Through these readings and practices, you will learn more about the heart of God, and be challenged to get to know God better.

Day 1

"Is Jesus real to me?"

Wesley's question, "Is Jesus real to me?" may be the most important question of all, because it's the question that's really at the heart of your faith. Another way to ask the question is, "Do you really know Jesus—like you know your best friend—or do you just know *about* Jesus?" There's a big difference between the two. Because having a relationship with Jesus and trusting him with your life is way more important than just knowing facts and rules *about the Christian religion*. Knowing a lot about Jesus might change what's going on in your head, but getting to know Jesus in a real way changes what's going on in your heart. And when Jesus is real to you, it encourages others to believe in him too.

Read Acts 8:25–40. This Scripture tells the story of an Ethiopian man and Philip, a disciple of Jesus. The Lord told Philip to travel down a certain road, where he ran into this man, who was trying to read Scripture but was having trouble understanding it. Philip helped the man make sense of what he was reading, and told him the good news about Jesus. As a result, the man trusted in Jesus and asked to be baptized as a believer and follower of Christ. Jesus was made real to the man that day.

Are you simply following a religion, or are you following Jesus? Do you have a relationship with Jesus? Jesus becomes more real to us each day when we spend time with him, and this happens when we commit to reading Scripture, praying, spending time with other believers, and spending quiet, unplugged time just listening for his voice. Philip listened, and when God said go, Philip went because Jesus was real to him, and Philip believed God could use him to spread the good news. As a result, another man's life was forever changed, and Philip's faith was no doubt strengthened.

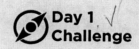

Day 1 Challenge

How might you make Jesus real for someone you come in contact with today? Ask the Lord to help you to notice the needs of people around you and to listen for God's voice to lead you. When you do hear from God, go, and be bold in showing others the love of Jesus.

Day 2

"Am I enjoying prayer?"

Day 2 Challenge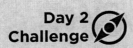

Create your own one-sentence prayer, such as "Lord God, be with me today and help me to show your love to others," or "I have faith; help my lack of faith!" (from Mark 9:24 CEB). Repeat the sentence throughout the day, saying it more than once each time you pray it.

What does it mean to "enjoy" prayer? To be honest, I've never really wondered if I am "enjoying" prayer. But the more I think about Wesley's question, the more important I think the question is for us.

To "enjoy" prayer is simply to have a good experience of prayer. Whether it is daily, hourly, or occasionally, prayer is meant to be a positive and enriching worship experience. Prayer isn't just another thing to put on our to-do lists. Prayer is an opportunity to have a powerful experience with God. To pray and enjoy it, then, is to regularly practice prayer and, as a result, to develop a deeper understanding of God, yourself, others, and the world.

Prayer is an experience with God, and that experience can include all kinds of emotions. For instance, have you ever cried out to God in anger? That is a prayer experience. Have you ever questioned God with a "Why?" That is also prayer. And even though the circumstances that led up to you crying out to God were likely not-great moments, they still led you to an experience with the Lord and you gave God the opportunity to speak to you.

Read John 17. I love this chapter, which is just Jesus praying. Within this prayer, I think we can gain insight and develop perspective about what Wesley meant when he asked the question, "Am I enjoying prayer?" We find that Jesus' prayer was meant to do four things. First, Jesus' prayer was meant to bring glory to God. Second, Jesus prays for himself and that through his actions he might bring glory to God. Third, Jesus prays for his friends, the disciples. Finally, Jesus prays for those yet to come, those who will be impacted by the ministry of the disciples as the Holy Spirit leads them. (Hint: That's you!) Jesus models for us that to "enjoy" prayer is to experience God by recognizing God, self, others, and the world, and at the same time trusting the direction God desires for our lives.

I believe there are at least five helpful ways that we can practice experiencing God through prayer:

1. Find a routine and a regular place to pray.
2. Schedule time(s) in the day to pray.
3. Pray with others and for others.
4. Memorize one-sentence prayers to help you pray when you're not sure what to pray.
5. Pray with a humble heart, acknowledging the Lord's authority in your life.

Day 3

"When my conscience tells me something is wrong, do I do it anyway?"

When I was a kid, I developed a very bad habit—I was a shoplifter. I stole the things I wanted but couldn't pay for. It got to be such a bad habit that nearly every time I walked into a store I would walk out with a toy, a game, a music CD, whatever I wanted. I knew it was wrong, but I did it anyway, even though I would get a funny feeling in the pit of my stomach. Eventually I got caught, and my secret came out. I know I am forgiven and that God's grace has given me freedom from those wrong choices, but I still get knots in my stomach when I talk about it, even all these years later. Those "knots in my stomach," I believe, are my conscience reminding me that what I did was wrong.

Last week I had a conversation with a friend who admitted a long-term addiction to pornography. As we talked about his damaging habit, he said, "I know it is wrong because every time I click on the websites I shouldn't

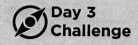 **Day 3 Challenge**

Do you have areas of your life that are causing you an uneasy conscience? What are these weaknesses? Tell a trusted friend or adult about a temptation you are struggling with. Ask for help and accountability in thinking through practical ways you can combat the temptations you are facing.

be looking at, I get an uneasy feeling. My conscience is telling me not to go there, but I do it anyway."

Read Ephesians 2:10. The feelings we get when we insist on doing harmful things—such as gossiping, lusting, lying, stealing, cheating, and so on—are the Holy Spirit reminding us that God created us to do good, not evil. That's why Bible reading and prayer are so important. Through these practices, God can shape our consciences and help us remember that God wants more for us—that we were created to do good things in God's name. Ignoring that gentle nudging from your conscience means you are deliberately choosing to ignore God's desire for your good.

Jeremiah 29:11 says, "'For I know the plans I have for you,' declares the LORD, 'plans to prosper you and not to harm you, plans to give you hope and a future'" (NIV). Although it can be annoying at times, an uneasy conscience can be a good thing because it reminds us that God loves us and wants the best for us.

Day 4

"Did the Bible live in me today?"

Day 4 Challenge

Keep a Bible with you at all times today. Let it remind you of God's desire to be with you in every moment of your day. When you have a few free moments, read Hebrews 4:12 again or another favorite verse. How is the Word living and active in you today?

Throughout much of my life, I've had a complicated relationship with the Bible. When I was a kid, I enjoyed the prizes I got for memorizing Bible verses and Bible stories. As a teenager, I viewed the Bible more as a rule book that was determined to keep me from having fun. And as a young adult in seminary, I considered the Bible a piece of great literature, full of ideas and philosophies that related to my purpose as a human being.

I've learned over the years, however, that the Bible's value does not come from the prizes you are awarded as a kid for memorizing it. It's also not a tool we use to control others. Or, it's not for use as a philosophy textbook. No, the Bible is a love story—the story of a loving, creative God who is good. It is a collection of wonderfully engaging stories, written through poetry, prophecy, and parables, meant not just to amuse or entertain, but to shape the very lives we live.

The Bible is the story of a people who were chosen by God and called to reveal God to the world. These people, as we see throughout Scripture, struggled to remain faithful to God, but God never gave up on them. When we engage the Bible through personal and group study, we encounter God. God inspired the Bible, meaning that God had an active role in shaping the Bible. The Bible reveals the human struggle and all that is wrong with humanity, while at the same time telling of God's enduring love that redeems us. When we read the Bible, we bring all of our experiences—our joys, concerns, celebrations, and struggles—to it, and the Bible meets us head on with God's promises of forgiveness and hope.

Read Hebrews 4:12. Wesley's question, "Did the Bible live in me today?" is profound because he didn't ask, "Did we read our Bible today?" but did it *live* in us? In other words, is the Bible actively shaping your heart, your inner self?

Day 5
"Did I disobey God in anything?"

When God created human beings, God did so with complete love, and that complete love gave humans complete freedom. God gave human beings the freedom to love God or not, to obey God or not. But to love God *is* to obey God, and to disobey God is to love yourself more than God. It might seem hard to imagine that a powerful, all-knowing God would create humans with such a personal power. But God understood that in order to love a person, there must be a real freedom for him or her to love you back or not. To be genuine, love must be mutual. God did not preprogram or hardwire humans with an obedience code. Instead, God created us with the ability to choose. The question is: Will we love ourselves above God (disobey) or will we love God above ourselves (obey)?

What does it mean to love God above yourself? Loving God above yourself means that you respect God's authority to lead and direct your life. It means that you choose God's desires over your own, even when it's really hard to do. It means that you believe God has your best in mind, and you commit to following God's way.

Day 5 Challenge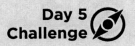

Spend a few minutes today reflecting on your life. In what areas of your life are you intentionally living for your own self rather than for God's glory?

Sometimes we disobey God by doing things God has specifically told us not to do. Other times we disobey God by doing nothing—by ignoring the things God has told us to do. Both are forms of disobedience. I believe God has equipped every one of us with the ability to choose to do what is right, even though living obedient lives is hard, and we mess up—a lot. But when we mess up, we confess that to God (and to others, if needed). We ask for God's forgiveness and give thanks that God's grace gives us a fresh start. Because God's love is greater than your mistakes.

Read Matthew 5:14-16. Jesus says that we are the light of the world, and choosing to obey God's desires for our lives means that through our obedient actions, we shine a light on God's goodness and grace for the world. It means that we value what God values, and we shine the light of God's love out to the world around us. Micah 6:8 says, "He has told you, O man, what is good; and what does the LORD require of you but to do justice, and to love kindness, and to walk humbly with your God?" (ESV). How is God calling you to obey today?

Day 6
"Do I pray about the money I spend?"

Now I know you might be thinking, "What money? I hardly have any!" But the truth is, whether you have a little money or a lot of money, what matters is your perspective on money and how you allow it to shape your life. Money in and of itself is not inherently bad, but the Bible says that it is the *love of* money that can distract and control us (see 1 Timothy 6:10).

Like many other things we struggle with, the love of money can get between us and God and can cause us to focus less on God and more on our own needs. Putting God first in our lives means that we view our money and possessions through God's eyes and that we ask God to guide us in the ways we use our money. We realize that everything is God's and that we are simply using God's money for the purposes of God's work in the world—to provide for our families, to feed the hungry and clothe the naked, to provide shelter for the homeless, and ultimately, to value the things that God values. That is why we take the time to consider how we get our money. We ask, "Am I harming someone else in order to make money?" That means we think about how we spend our money. We ask, "Do I waste money on things I don't really need or spend more than I can afford?" That means we strive to give generously where we can and where God leads us to give. We ask, "Where can I step into what God is already doing and use my money for good?"

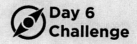

Day 6 Challenge

Put a little money in your pocket or purse today, and determine that you will use it to help someone else. Pray for God to give you eyes to see the people around with a new perspective and to lead you in how you spend your money. And when you hear from God, don't second-guess it. Act on it!

Jesus said: "Do not store up for yourselves treasures on earth, where moths and vermin destroy, and where thieves break in and steal. But store up for yourselves treasures in heaven, where moths and vermin do not destroy, and where thieves do not break in and steal. For where your treasure is, there your heart will be also" (Matthew 6:19-21). Here Jesus encourages us not to spend our lives in pursuit of getting more and more money and physical things for ourselves, but to realize that the things that are really worth our time and effort are the things that God values. When we seek God's plans for how we use our money, we are able to see that the needs of others are just as important as our own, and we will desire to give as God leads us.

Day 7

"Do I give time for the Bible to speak to me every day?"

God can speak to us anytime and anywhere. God wants to communicate God's love to us, so God uses lots of things to speak to us—sometimes we hear God's voice through other people or music or prayer or creation or circumstances that come our way. We also hear God speak through the Bible, God's Holy Word.

But what does it mean to allow the Bible to "speak" to us? It might sound quirky or even weird to think about the Bible "speaking," but here's what I mean by that:

Day 7 Challenge

Devote twenty minutes today to reading one of the Gospel stories, such as when Jesus calms the storm in Mark 4:35-41. Approach the time with an open mind and heart. Listen for God's voice as you read and think about what you've read. What did you hear from God today?

- God makes truth known by **revealing** it to us through the Bible. When we say God inspired the Bible, we mean God intentionally gave us the Bible by collaborating with human authors to help us know who God is and what God is like.
- When God makes truth known, God also gives us **understanding** of the truth. The ministry of the Holy Spirit is to take truth from the Bible and allow us to comprehend it. Our minds and hearts are shaped when the Spirit lights up the Bible. Then it "speaks" to us.
- God reveals truth to us, helps us to understand it, and then fires our **imagination**, giving us ways to live out truth and share it with others. When God fires our imaginations, God gives us opportunities to actively participate with God's work in the world.

In order to allow God to speak to us through the Bible, we must develop the discipline of regular Bible reading and study. Although many of us struggle to find the time, reading the Bible is essential to growing in our Christian faith. Wesley asks this question—"Do I give time for the Bible to speak to me every day?"—not to just create more for Christians to do, but to point out the importance of taking the time to let God speak to us through God's Word. Bible reading is not simply a task to be completed; it is a practice to shape us and mold us into who God invites us to be.

It's important to remember that we do not put our faith in the Bible—we put our faith in the God of the Bible. Simply put, the Bible gives us wisdom to help us grow as believers in our faith. When you take the time to come to the Bible to listen, knowing that you have more to learn, and ready to act when God leads you, you create more opportunity for God to speak to you, and you will grow in your relationship with God.

Going Deeper

When you hear the word *discipline*, what images come to mind? Most likely, they aren't pleasant images. If we're honest, none of us would probably say that we love to be disciplined in our lives. We like to be good at stuff, but we don't love to practice. We want the results, but putting in the time to get those results often feels tedious and boring. But putting that daily time and effort into your music or sports or art is what really makes the difference, and the same is true in your relationship with God.

Are you putting in the time with God in order to know God better? For example, when God speaks to you about your thoughts or actions, do you hear it? When God challenges you about the ways you're spending your money or using the resources you've been given, do you hear God's voice? When God says go, are you open and eager?

In order to have a deep relationship with God, the daily stuff—praying and reading and studying the Bible is important. Why? Because in order to have a real relationship with God, we need to practice. We need to practice listening for God, and these are some of the most important ways we can do that. Having a real relationship with God means that we submit all areas of our hearts and lives to God and ask God to guide us in all those areas. It means that we realize that God is the one who helps us thrive and grow and that we can't do it on our own. Jesus said:

> "I am the Real Vine and my Father is the Farmer. He cuts off every branch of me that doesn't bear grapes. And every branch that is grape-bearing he prunes back so it will bear even more. You are already pruned back by the message I have spoken.
>
> Live in me. Make your home in me just as I do in you. In the same way that a branch can't bear grapes by itself but only by being joined to the vine, you can't bear fruit unless you are joined with me.

23

> I am the Vine, you are the branches. When you're joined with me and I with you, the relation intimate and organic, the harvest is sure to be abundant. Separated, you can't produce a thing."
>
> John 15:1–8 MSG

Our relationship with God is the most important and rewarding relationship of our lives, and it's worth everything we can give to it, because God gave everything for that relationship to happen: "For God so loved the world that he gave his one and only Son, that whoever believes in him shall not perish but have eternal life" (John 3:16).

How is God trying to draw you closer today? How is your spiritual growth? Is it time to step it up and add in some more practices that might deepen and enrich your faith?

Sharing Thoughts and Feelings

Spend some time with a group discussing these questions.

- Would you say that Jesus is "real" to you? If so, in what areas do you most feel Jesus' presence or influence in your life? If not, what do you think is standing in the way of your having a close relationship with Jesus? Are there any doubts or struggles you need to face?
- What do you think it means to have a healthy and impactful life of prayer? How's your prayer life? Do you currently have a routine or schedule for praying and listening to God? As Wesley asked, do you "enjoy" prayer? What obstacles do you face in praying? What encourages you the most when you pray?
- When you hear the word conscience, what images come to mind? What kind of relationship do you have with your conscience? Do you tend to listen to it or ignore it? How do you respond to correction by God or by trusted people in your life?
- How important is the Bible to a Christian? What's your relationship with the Bible right now? How much time do you spend in the Bible, and do you make it a priority in your life? What obstacles are standing in your way in regard to reading and studying the Bible?

- Of Wesley's seven questions asked this week, which had the most impact on you, and why?

Doing Things Together

Making Jesus Real in a New Way
Supplies: Poster or markerboard, marker

Sometimes we get so caught up in our day-to-day lives that we fail to think about how Jesus can play an active role in how we live. Seeing the world from a different perspective by shaking up our routines can often open our eyes to live a vibrant life with Jesus and serve others too.

Using a posterboard or markerboard, brainstorm ways you might shake up your usual life experiences and routines in order to see Jesus in a new way. You might choose one practice that you don't typically engage in, such as fasting, or you might think about heading out together, field-trip style, to serve at a homeless shelter or children's home. You might collect and deliver donations for a local organization that can use the help. Or go to an event such as The Compassion Experience (compassion.com/change), which gives you a glimpse into what people's lives look like who live in developing countries around the world. (Hint: A lot of people's lives look really different from yours.)

Commit to one of these shake-ups in your daily life, or plan a future group outing to one of the places you've chosen. As you are doing these activities, ask, what would Jesus mean to me if I was in this situation? How does this change my perspective on Jesus? How does it change my relationship with Jesus?

Seeing the Bible with New Eyes
Supplies: Bible, pen/pencil, and paper

1. Think about one of the Bible stories you learned as a child (such as the story of Noah's ark or Daniel in the lions' den). Without looking it up, write down the key elements of the story as you remember them. Try to recall what your main understanding of the story was when you first encountered it.
2. Next, pull out your Bible or use an online Bible resource and read the story now. What parts of the story seem new or different to you? What do you understand about the story now

that you didn't really understand as a child? How has your life experience changed or deepened your understanding of God's Word?

As a pair or group, make a commitment to study the Bible together daily. One easy way to do this is to sign up to have a daily devotional sent to your phone or email. Start your day by reading that devotional and giving yourself time to process its meaning for you. Make a plan for holding each other accountable to the practice, and talk together about what you're learning.

Listening for God

Read and pray these words, as Jesus directed:

"With a God like this loving you, you can pray very simply. Like this:

> Our Father in heaven,
> Reveal who you are.
> Set the world right;
> Do what's best—
>   as above, so below.
> Keep us alive with three square meals.
> Keep us forgiven with you and forgiving others.
> Keep us safe from ourselves and the Devil.
> You're in charge!
> You can do anything you want!
> You're ablaze in beauty!
>   Yes. Yes. Yes."

Matthew 6: 9–13 MSG

Notes and Thoughts Week 1

Week 2
RELATIONSHIP WITH SELF: AN INWARD FOCUS

You are the one who created my innermost parts;
  you knit me together while I was still in my
  mother's womb.
I give thanks to you that I was marvelously set
apart.
  Your works are wonderful—I know that
  very well.

                    Psalm 139:13-14 CEB

Week 2

RELATIONSHIP WITH SELF: AN INWARD FOCUS

In order to grow in our relationship with God, we must know ourselves well. We need to take the time to do the hard work of looking inside to see what's going on in our hearts and minds in order to mature and grow in our faith—not to be afraid to look deep into our souls, reflect upon what paths our lives are on, and make the necessary changes to become who God created us to be.

Wesley knew that in order to fully live into our God-intended design, we must be people whose inner lives match our outer lives. And so Wesley gave us seven questions that lead us toward discovering our true self. As we read these questions, we have to be honest with ourselves. This doesn't mean we beat ourselves up for all our weaknesses and shortcomings—instead we look inside with the knowledge that God loves us as we are and that we cannot earn God's love by doing anything because that love is freely given to us. When we really know our value and worth in God's eyes, we want to become the people God intends for us to be.

This week's questions are meant to help us become the men and women God intends for us to be. They are intended to help us look within, to see if there is anything standing in the way of a deeper, fuller relationship with God and with others. So let's dig deep, with the full assurance that God's got us, no matter what!

Day 8
"Am I proud?"

Day 8 Challenge

Ask a trusted friend or mentor to share his or her opinion of your three biggest strengths and three biggest areas of improvement. Pray about the response, and ask the Lord to change your perspective on your life and what God wants to do in it.

Contributed by Chris Abel

Have you ever stood beneath a clear, starry sky and felt that you were a very small speck in a very big universe? News flash: you are indeed a very small speck in a very big universe. In 1990, the Voyager 1 space probe took a photo of Earth from 3.7 billion miles away, and from its position, all that could be seen of our planet was a tiny speck of light in a vast sea of darkness. Astronomer Carl Sagan famously called it the "pale blue dot." You and I live on this "pale blue dot," but unlike the Voyager 1 space probe, we don't have access to this perspective. We don't have the privilege of seeing our lives from the far reaches of space. We live very much on the surface of that dot. We live our one human life, eyes close to the ground, caught up in our day-to-day busyness. And from that perspective, the small things in life often feel like big things.

Even though we humans are a very small part of something very, very big, there's a temptation to think very highly of ourselves. We all know those people who walk around as if they own the school. Sometimes, *we're* even those people! Saint Augustine once said that pride is "the love of one's own excellence." We're not talking about a healthy self-esteem here—we're talking about a perspective that says we are somehow superior to others. We all do this in some way, taking little parts of our lives and feeling pride about them. Maybe your good grades make you feel superior to others. Or maybe the fact that you don't care about your grades makes you feel superior to those who work hard for them. Maybe you feel superior to others because you dress better or have more things or spend more hours volunteering in your community. We can literally be prideful about *anything*.

When your head and your heart are focused only on your own life, you will naturally struggle with pride. When your energy, time, and thoughts revolve mostly around your life, your concerns, and your comfort—you will absolutely feel superior to others. After all, you are living as if you're the center of the universe! Lucky for us, God isn't bound by our perspective. The God of the universe sees us as we are—limited but beautiful, flawed yet full of amazing potential.

Read John 3:1-21, in which Jesus has a conversation with a Jewish teacher named Nicodemus. Nicodemus has every right to be proud. He is a very respected teacher, and yet he's curious about Jesus' teachings. And so Jesus says to him, "I assure you, unless someone is born anew, it's not possible to see God's kingdom" (John 3:3 CEB). The study notes in my Bible define *anew* as "from above." When you're too close to the ground, you can't see the kingdom of God and God's purpose for us. Jesus teaches us to live our lives from *above*. Just like seeing a city from an airplane, when we are born from above, we get a different perspective on what God is doing in the world. And when we have a higher perspective, it's hard to feel pride about something so small, isn't it?

Day 9
"Am I defeated in any part of my life?"

We all experience times in our lives when we feel defeated, overcome with emotions or feelings or stress. And if we don't acknowledge these feelings, or ask for help, it affects us mentally, physically, emotionally, and spiritually. This happens to all of us, and when it does, we need people in our lives to help us get through it because we are meant to live life with the help, encouragement, and support of others.

Why is it often so hard for us to be honest about needing help? More often than not, we feel we need to put on a mask that makes everything seem OK even when it isn't. But a strong person admits the need for help and calls out for it. We are not failures because we are failing at something. Our strength does

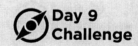

Day 9 Challenge

Confide in someone close to you any areas in your life in which that you are feeling defeated, and ask for prayer and help. Be specific. Then read Isaiah 43:1-8, and reflect on what it means to draw on God's strength in your life.

not reside in our own self—our strength comes from God, the source of all of strength and life itself.

To admit that we are defeated is an act of courage. To admit that we need help is bravery. To admit that our stability and strength come from God is an act of worship because we honor God when we declare our need for God's help. (The Book of Psalms, along with many books in the Old Testament, are filled with constant cries for help and support.).

Again, it is OK to feel defeated and down sometimes, so when you do, have the courage to admit it, and surround yourself with people who love and support you and remind you of God's goodness in your life. God desires that we live joyful lives and that our joy be found in God's goodness and gifts of life. God generously gives us gifts like grace, mercy, forgiveness, hope, faithfulness, and peace. To experience these gifts fully we need to place our full trust in God's strength, not in our own.

Day 10

"Do I go to bed on time and get up on time?"

OK, so it seems like Wesley is switching gears here a little bit. First we're talking about our deepest struggles, and now we're moving on to our...sleep habits?

I think if Wesley were alive today and proposing this question, he would help us see that it isn't just about going to bed on time and getting up on time. I think he would help us wrestle with what it means to be in good health (spiritually, physically, socially, financially) overall, and his question would also get at our willingness to live a disciplined life in general.

We all know the benefits of being well rested. Some of these include being more joyful the next day, having a clearer mind, driving more safely, making better decisions, and experiencing an overall optimistic outlook on life. When I don't go to bed on time and wake up on time, I am grumpy, my mind is cluttered, I am lethargic and sluggish, and I walk around like I am in a fog. This means I am missing opportunities to go where God is leading me throughout my day.

Read Mark 1:29-39. Here we see Jesus engaged in God's work of healing those who were ill. The scriptures indicate that "the whole town" gathered at the door of the house where Jesus was staying, and throughout the night Jesus healed many. After Jesus had healed many, we see him choosing to find a solitary place where he can be renewed. Mark 1:35 says, "Very early in the morning, while it was still dark, Jesus got up, left the house and went off to a solitary place where he prayed." To be in good health may not only require a full night's rest—it may also require times of solitude.

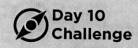

Day 10 Challenge

What can you do today to renew yourself so that you are ready to encourage those you will interact with today?

Jesus knew the importance of finding the time to be renewed in order that he might remain focused on the mission at hand. This is what Wesley is encouraging us to do. What do we need to do to be our best? What do we need to do to stay healthy, so that whatever we do, we do it faithfully? We represent God and by working hard we bring honor to God. When we are rested and at our best, we can be sure to find ways to participate in God's mission for the world around us.

Wesley wants us to realize when asking us this simple question. "Do we go to bed on time and get up on time?" that it is code for "Are you rested and at your best so that you can meet the challenges of the day and ultimately help make the world a better place?"

Day 11

"Do I grumble or complain constantly?"

We all know that person in our family, friend group, or school who always seems to be complaining about something. (Maybe it's even us. *Cringe.*) People grumble for a lot of reasons, but I think people mostly complain because they haven't yet discovered what it means to be content. People who complain and aren't content with life are not able to live at peace with themselves and typically blame everyone else for their circumstances.

The Israelites were constantly complaining when Moses was leading them during their years of wandering in the desert. God had freed them from slavery, and yet they said they'd rather return to Egypt because at least there they had more comforts and food options. Seriously? Did they really want to go back into slavery? Probably not, but they

Day 11 Challenge

Read Philippians 2:14-16. Pay attention to your urge to complain throughout the day. When you find yourself on the verge of grumbling, stop yourself and ask what would be gained by your complaining. Ask what might be gained by your positivity.

were discontented with their situation. Their momentary, selfish, personal desires overshadowed the monumental thing God had done in freeing them.

Complainers are not bad people. Often they just need an attitude adjustment. When we are able to practice and learn to be content or satisfied, we change the patterns of negativity in our lives into more positive ones. We gain a more optimistic outlook on life when we avoid complaining.

Wesley wanted fellow believers to ask one another this question—"Do I grumble or complain constantly?"—so that we can become aware of unintentional patterns or habits we might have formed in this area. We ask this question of ourselves and each other so that we can work to replace our negative thoughts with positive thoughts and start developing new habits marked by hope and optimism. What's more, we need to ask this question so that we take responsibility for our role in the circumstances that come our way and step up to participate in God's work, cheerfully and with joy. The good news of Jesus is good for a reason, after all! Let's be people who seek to choose joy over misery and to reveal the good news of Jesus through our contentment and gratitude for what he has done for us.

Day 12

"Am I a slave to dress, friends, work, or habits?"

What motivates and controls you? I believe the underlying principle behind today's question from Wesley is this: Who or what owns us? What consumes us? Who or what do we allow to control our lives?

When we are "slaves" to something or someone, it means that we take our direction from a person or object that is not God, and these things, such as possessions, money, or popularity gives us a false sense of freedom. When we are slaves to dress, friends, work, habits, or any other controlling factor, we allow ourselves to love earthly things, which leads us into a deeper love for what pleases us rather than what pleases God. Sometimes it isn't about material possessions such as clothes or cars or the newest phone. Sometimes we are slaves to our image. We want to be seen as fun, beautiful, successful, or influential. We spend hours on social media, trying to build a name for ourselves. We want to rack up the "likes" and can't get enough approval from our friends and classmates. This need for affirmation can consume us, and in pursuing it, we can become a slave to it.

The fundamental inner battle each of us faces as a Christian is the battle between giving ourselves over to God's mission or living a life based on our own plan. So how can we intentionally choose God's mission over our own desires? Here are a few ideas:

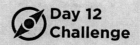 **Day 12 Challenge**

Pay attention to the messages you receive from your social media feeds, from your entertainment sources, and from the circle of your closest friends and acquaintances. Note how these messages might be influencing you to place possessions ahead of what God desires for you.

Observe and record your impulses. When you feel yourself being pulled toward a certain vice such as social media, shopping, overeating, working out, studying, or something else, write it down. Recording it gives you a chance to look back and observe what pulls you and when. Then, as you understand why you desire that thing, you can more effectively avoid it pulling you in.

Find a place to serve. One of the best ways to focus on God's mission for you is to serve others. Find a place where you can focus on others and their needs instead of your own desires.

Think *people over possessions.* When we focus too heavily on possessions, we can forget to value the people around us. We all know that people matter more than the things we own, so make an effort to use your energy first and foremost on the people God has put into your life.

As believers, we are called out of being slaves to what keeps us from loving God and loving others. We are called toward a healthy, balanced life of serving God and others.

Day 13

"How do I spend my spare time?"

Day 13 Challenge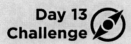

As your day unfolds, pay attention to how you fill your spare time. Record that information honestly, and review it at the end of the day. Did you have more or less spare time than you anticipated? How do you feel about how you spent that time?

"There's never enough time!" We all say this, but is it actually true? It *is* true that there are lots of things competing for our time. Between school and work and sports and theater and home life, our minutes and hours and days are eaten up by a million different things. But in order to be good stewards of the time we've been given, it's essential for us to consider the way we spend our time, especially our spare (or free) time.

Take a few minutes to think about and possibly journal about where your time goes in an ordinary day. How much free time do you think you have to spend? What do you typically do with that time?

Wesley could have asked this question for many reasons, but let's consider two possible reasons he'd want us to consider this issue. First, we are all busy and juggling many demands on our time, so it's essential that we set aside time to renew and refresh ourselves. What activities or hobbies are fun for you and make you feel the most refreshed and energized? When we pursue these things, it helps us reset and reboot. It helps us relax and refocus our energies on what is essential for us and what is not. How much of your spare time do you spend engaged in these kinds of life-giving activities? If it's less than you would like, how can you restructure your time so that you are spending it in ways that bring you life and joy? I don't think Wesley (or Jesus, for that matter) cares how we spend our spare time, as long as it enriches our lives and maybe even the lives of others around us.

A second reason we should consider how we spend our spare time is that it often reveals what we value in life. What does your spare time tell you about what you love? When you have a little downtime, where do you automatically go? Do you immediately go to your phone, to social media? Do you plop down in front of the TV or computer to watch a show? We all need a little mindless downtime here and there, but if this is your first go-to, it's important to ask, "Is this the *best* way to refresh myself? Is this filling me up in a way that's renewing me?"

It's also helpful to consider your spare time to ask if you're spending time with the Lord and in God's Word. Read Matthew 6:21. Do you find it easy to fill your spare time with hobbies and activities, but find it hard to make the time to spend with the Lord? How might you need to reorder your priorities so that you're making time to hear from God? What might the Lord be saying to you about the time you've been given?

Day 14
"Am I self-conscious, self-pitying, or self-justifying?"

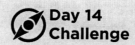
Day 14 Challenge

It is healthy to be self-aware. When we know ourselves well, it helps us navigate decisions, avoid giving in to temptations, carefully responding to people we disagree with, and knowing the areas in which we need help or support. Generally speaking, knowing ourselves well helps us live a balanced life. But if we're not careful, being too self-aware can make us self-absorbed. Wesley wants us to consider the question, "Am I self-conscious, self-pitying, or self-justifying?" so that we recognize our human tendency to be so concerned with "self" that we lose sight of the "others" in our lives.

Read Genesis 3. In the story of Adam and Eve, we see them disobeying God and trying to pin it on someone else. This human desire to blame others comes from self-absorption, from wanting to protect ourselves first,

Do something outside of your comfort zone today—something that makes you a little nervous and uncomfortable. Talk to a stranger, invite someone you don't know well to eat lunch, take treats to the neighbors who keep to themselves. Think of a way to reach out and serve others.

no matter the costs. None of us is exempt from these feelings and behaviors—at one time or another, we've all given in to the temptation to think of ourselves, and only ourselves, first. So how can we combat self-centeredness? Here are a few things to try:

1. Volunteer and serve others.
2. Engage in random acts of kindness.
3. Practice empathy by really listening to another person's story.
4. Find something you don't think you'll be great at, and do it anyway.
5. Do something that takes you out of your normal routine or comfort zone.
6. If you like to be the one in control, let someone else lead for once.
7. Make an effort to get to know someone you find hard to like.

Wesley does us a favor by asking us this question, because this question reminds us to take the focus off of ourselves and put it on God and God's mission for our world. It helps us be aware of our faults and shortcomings and tendencies, but reminds us that God is bigger than whatever good or bad we bring into the world. God's got this, and we are blessed to play our part.

Going Deeper

No matter where you go or what you do, there is one person in the world who you will never be able to avoid—you. Love it or hate it, you're stuck with yourself, and that is something that will never, ever change. Thankfully, we have Someone who helps us navigate our hearts.

The God of the universe made you with precision and purpose and sticks with you always. In Psalm 139, the psalmist celebrates how the Lord has created him and wants to have a relationship with him:

God, investigate my life;
    get all the facts firsthand.

I'm an open book to you;
>
> even from a distance, you know what I'm thinking.

You know when I leave and when I get back;
>
> I'm never out of your sight.

You know everything I'm going to say
>
> before I start the first sentence.

I look behind me and you're there,
>
> then up ahead and you're there, too—
>
> your reassuring presence, coming and going.

This is too much, too wonderful—
>
> I can't take it all in! . . .

Oh yes, you shaped me first inside, then out;
>
> you formed me in my mother's womb.

I thank you, High God—you're breathtaking!
>
> Body and soul, I am marvelously made!
>
> I worship in adoration—what a creation!

You know me inside and out,
>
> you know every bone in my body;

You know exactly how I was made, bit by bit,
>
> how I was sculpted from nothing into something.

Like an open book, you watched me grow from conception to birth;
>
> all the stages of my life were spread out before you,

The days of my life all prepared
>
> before I'd even lived one day. . . .

Investigate my life, O God,
>
> find out everything about me;

Cross-examine and test me,
>
> get a clear picture of what I'm about;

See for yourself whether I've done anything wrong—
>
> then guide me on the road to eternal life.

Psalm 139:1-6, 13-16, 23-24 MSG

Can you hear the psalmist's enthusiasm for himself, as a creation of the Lord? God doesn't make mistakes, and God didn't make a mistake in creating you. Yes, we humans are fickle and fragile and often do the wrong thing, but we were created in the image of God, and God has a plan for us. And so regularly looking into your heart to see what is standing in the way of your relationship with God and with others only helps you better participate in God's mission on earth. Taking an honest look at how you spend your time, what motivates you, what controls you, and how you live your day-to-day life helps you see the areas that need adjustments.

In what areas of your life is God calling you to take a closer look and make some changes? What do you need to take a deeper look at in your life so that you can be more available and willing to be a part of what God is up to in the world around you?

Sharing Thoughts and Feelings

Spend some time with a group discussing these questions.

- What do you think it means to be proud? What are some things that people around you seem to take pride in? Is there something that you have been prideful about, something that makes you feel better than other people?

- When you feel defeated about something, what is your go-to response? How does talking with other people about your struggles make you feel less alone in them? Is it easy or hard for you to ask for help?

- Think about a time you've felt exhausted and depleted. What was your behavior like at that time? What can you learn from that time, and how can you make changes to avoid that happening in the future?

- When something goes wrong, what is your natural response? Do you tend to be optimistic or pessimistic? Do you think you can change your basic nature in that respect?

- Do you know someone who is noticeably enslaved by possessions or obsessions? What effect is this having on that person's life or his or her family's life?

- How often do you attempt something you will be "bad" at? If your answer is "almost never," why do you think that is? What could change your outlook on that?

Doing Things Together

Discovering Who God Is

Supplies: *Posterboard or whiteboard and markers, pen or pencil and paper for each participant*

Read the following verses aloud. As you read, on a markerboard or large sheet of paper, make a list of God's traits, such as strength, goodness, power, and so on.

- Psalm 18:2 (CEB)
The LORD is my solid rock,
  my fortress, my rescuer.
My God is my rock—
I take refuge in him! —
  he's my shield,
  my salvation's strength,
  my place of safety.

- John 16:33 (CEB)
I've said these things to you so that you will have peace in me. In the world you have distress. But be encouraged! I have conquered the world.

- Matthew 19:26
Jesus looked at them and said, "With men this is impossible, but with God all things are possible."

- 2 Timothy 1:7 (NKJV)
For God has not given us a spirit of fear, but of power and of love and of a sound mind.

- Psalm 46:1 (NKJV)
God *is* our refuge and strength,
a very present help in trouble.

- Hebrews 4:15-16 (NKJV)
For we do not have a High Priest who cannot sympathize with our weaknesses, but was in all *points* tempted as *we are*, *yet* without sin. Let us therefore come boldly to the throne of

grace, that we may obtain mercy and find grace to help in time of need.

- Romans 8:37-39 (NKJV)

Yet in all these things we are more than conquerors through Him who loved us. For I am persuaded that neither death nor life, nor angels nor principalities nor powers, nor things present nor things to come, nor height nor depth, nor any other created thing, shall be able to separate us from the love of God which is in Christ Jesus our Lord.

Discuss:

- Which of these traits or verses speaks to you most right now in your life?
- How can you claim these characteristics of God in what you're facing right now?

Write down one verse or trait of God on a piece of paper, and keep it in your car, purse, wallet, or somewhere else you will see it throughout the week and be reminded of God's strength and power and how we are free to ask God to be with us in our struggles.

Reboot Your Life
Supplies: Paper and pen or pencil for each participant

All of the questions we've considered this week have been aimed at making you rethink your life and how you spend it. We've asked: What refreshes you and gets you excited? What motivates you? What challenges you? What pushes you to think outside your own little corner of the world?

Quietly consider the questions below and take a few minutes to write down your answers.

- What is something I could do this week in my spare time that would be fun for me?
- What is one way I could serve someone else this week?
- What is one thing I can do this week that is out of my comfort zone? (This should be something that challenges you—maybe even something you're "bad" at—but you commit to doing it anyway.)

Share your answers aloud, and have someone else hold you accountable to do at least one of these things this week. When you do it, call, text, or e-mail that person to tell him or her about what you did and how it turned out. Encourage each other to keep pushing yourselves and see how God is revealed in the process.

Listening for God

God, teach me to serve you first and to seek your kingdom. Help me to be less concerned about myself and more interested in you and your mission for this world. Help me to be aware of myself, my faults, and my limitations, but also not to be so concerned with myself that I forget your purpose for me. In Jesus' name. Amen.

Notes and Thoughts for Week 2

Week 3

RELATIONSHIP WITH OTHERS: AN OUTWARD FOCUS

One of the teachers of the law came and heard them debating. Noticing that Jesus had given them a good answer, he asked him, "Of all the commandments, which is the most important?"

"The most important one," answered Jesus, "is this: 'Hear, O Israel: The Lord our God, the Lord is one. Love the Lord your God with all your heart and with all your soul and with all your mind and with all your strength.' The second is this: 'Love your neighbor as yourself.' There is no commandment greater than these."

Mark 12:28-31

Week 3

RELATIONSHIP WITH OTHERS: AN OUTWARD FOCUS

Throughout the Gospels, Jesus teaches us that the way we treat others is a direct reflection of our love for him. That means that if we practice our love for God, then we must pay careful attention to how we think about and interact with others, because to neglect or mistreat others is to neglect and mistreat Jesus.

This week Wesley's questions will challenge us to think beyond ourselves and ask us to consider the way we treat others. How we live life with others is clearly important to God's plan for our world. Verse after verse tells us to love our neighbor (Mark 12:31), to treat others with respect and encourage them (Ephesians 4:29), and to care for those who need our help (James 1:27). Sometimes the most impactful ways we can participate in God's mission is to make sure that the relationships in our homes, churches, schools, and communities follow the Bible's commands about how to treat one another.

As Christians who seek to obey God by loving others, we must work toward creating relationships that are honoring to God. Bottom line? The way we treat others matters because they, too, are treasured children of God. As you read, reflect, and pray in the coming days, be sure to remember that the biggest impact we can make in the whole world around us is often to the people right in front of us.

Day 15

"Do I thank God that I am not like others?"

Day 15 Challenge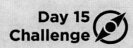

Count the number of times you compare yourself to others today. (Once you pay attention, you may be shocked at what you think!) Ask the Lord to forgive you and show you a new way forward.

We human beings are *really* good at comparing ourselves to one another. Like, *really good* at it. For example, spend two minutes on social media and consider what thoughts come to your mind in that very short time. Maybe it's something like, *I'm not as pretty as her. He posts too much—he is so full of himself. She thinks her life is so perfect.* Too often we tend to judge our own self-worth by others' situations, but the Bible tells us that comparing ourselves to others is dangerous business.

In Luke 18:9-14, Jesus told a story of two men who went to the temple to pray. The first man, a religious leader, demonstrated his love for God by naming all of the things he was doing right. Basically, this man was telling God why God should love him back. A second man, a not-so-popular tax collector, entered the temple to pray. This man was the opposite of the man described above. He was humble, sincere, and aware of his weaknesses. He came before God with a deep sense of grief and sorrow. This man, unlike the first one, recognized his sin and presented himself to God, aware of God's great might and glory. Which man's prayers do you think Jesus valued more? Jesus said, "This tax man, not the other, went home made right with God. If you walk around with your nose in the air, you're going to end up flat on your face, but if you're content to be simply yourself, you will become more than yourself" (v. 14 MSG).

There are many insights to be drawn from Jesus' story, but one is certainly that we are not to compare ourselves to others. We are to evaluate our own spiritual maturity based on what God desires from us, not from how much more "holy" we are than someone else. God doesn't desire our being better than another. Rather, God desires that we become the best possible individuals God has created us to be. We all have our junk, our issues, but when we come before God with a humble heart, not judging others but realizing our own sin and asking for help, God answers us and forgives us, leading us deeper into God's grace and mercy—for ourselves and for others.

Day 16

"Am I consciously or unconsciously creating the impression that I am better than I am? In other words, am I a hypocrite?"

Contributed by Chris Abel

So often in life, we struggle with appearances. We can't bear to have someone talk badly about us. We need to be liked. We dress to create a persona that more people will find attractive. We create piles of wealth, hoping that perhaps our finances might make us important. We strive to be seen as smart/creative/athletic/artistic. The list goes on. We attempt to "fake it 'til we make it."

The danger is that in doing so we create a fake life. We adopt an image that's not really us. We play the roles we feel others want us to play, all the while we're living frustrated and empty because we're denying who we really are. That's not living. That's not life. We often fake it to earn the love and approval of others, but even if we do earn it, what's it worth if it's . . . fake?

God doesn't want the fake you. God wants the *real* you, the authentic, flawed version of you. God doesn't need you to be perfect or have it all figured out. God isn't interested in judging or blaming. God is interested in your growth.

And when you are able to live in this version of yourself, you will be free. You will be free from living a life of constantly seeking others' approval. You will be able to handle criticism. You will be able to own your mistakes. You will be able to grow. Growth cannot come from faking it. When you're honest with yourself and others, you open the door to growth and begin to tap into the potential that God has in store for you. When you're honest with yourself, you stop faking it and start moving toward something greater. This is why *grace* is so powerful. It means that God isn't interested in blame or shame. God forgives because God wants you to be the fullest, most alive version of yourself.

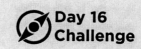

Day 16 Challenge

Read 2 Timothy 1:7. Ask someone you trust to name an area of your life in which you might be "faking it." How can you, with God's help, be more honest with yourself and others?

Wesley believed that God can do amazing things in our lives. He believed that we have incredible, God-given potential and are not slaves to our flaws and selfish inclinations. This process is called *sanctification*. It will take time and work, but God wants you to face yourself as you truly are because it is the doorway to seeing *who you can become*.

You have incredible potential. This is why you don't need to fake it. This is why you don't need to create an impression that you are better than you are. You, as you are, with all your cracks and flaws and blemishes, are amazing in God's eyes.

Day 17
"Am I a person who can be trusted?"

The basis of any good relationship is trust. Trust is the complete confidence that you can depend on someone else to keep your best in mind and that you feel safe and cared for by that person. Trust is the key to any and all healthy relationships, and trust has to be protected.

Recently my friend (let's call him Roger) wanted to talk to me about how to rebuild his relationship with his friend and business partner (let's call him Gary). Roger and Gary were lifelong friends, having grown up together in a small, rural Kansas town. They saw each other every day for years. Turns out that Roger had revealed to others some personal information Gary shared with him. The last time I saw Roger, the two hadn't spoken in months, they had sold the business, and their once-close families hadn't been together in ages. Breaking Gary's trust had destroyed their friendship.

I have shared personal and intimate matters of my life with others, in what I thought was complete confidence, only to have that information become public. You've probably had this happen too. And when this happens, it can destroy the relationship because trust is the foundation for strong, lasting relationships. So why do we sometimes feel compelled to share matters told to us in confidence? I think it's simple, really. We feel the need to relay private information because information is power. Humans love power, and we love to let others know that we have access to powerful information. (Remember how we also love to compare ourselves with one another?) By proving that we are "in the know," we may feel powerful at first, but that feeling soon gives way to feelings of guilt over what we've shared, knowing that we have hurt someone who trusted us.

Yet it is important to say that there are times when confidential matters *should* be shared with a trusted adult. If someone is being harmed, or is harming another, that information should not be kept secret. I was once asked to keep a secret of a friend who told me he was an alcoholic and that his disease had gotten so out of control that he was driving while intoxicated nearly every time he got in a car. This was not something to keep confidential. In order to protect my friend and others, I couldn't keep that secret.

Read Ephesians 4:29. God calls us into biblical community, and that means respecting the thoughts, feelings, and struggles of one

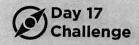

Day 17 Challenge

Think of the most trusted friend you have, and take time today to thank this person for being someone you can trust. Tell this person of the value you place on such presence in your life, and ask yourself if you are that kind of friend to others.

another, and supporting them in love. When we break trust by sharing information told to us in confidence, we damage our character. When we damage our character, we work against God's design for a good world. When we work to become holy people with integrity, trustworthiness, and reliability, we reveal Jesus Christ to the world around us.

Day 18

"Am I jealous, impure, critical, irritable, touchy, or distrustful?"

Wesley didn't beat around the bush, did he? If I am honest, my answer to the above question is a disheartening, "Yes." I don't like that I possess these types of behavior, but I do. Here are a few other ways to phrase the question: Do I want things that others have? Do I let my feelings sometimes ruin my day, and in some cases, another person's day as well? Do I criticize things that are not even my responsibility, and in some cases don't even affect me personally? Why do I make quick, hurtful remarks to my parents or siblings? Am I allowing my circumstances and situations to direct my behavior?

Day 18 Challenge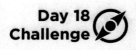

Force yourself to pause when an event or conversation triggers an emotional response in you. Take a deep breath and delay, asking the Lord to be with you. You might even pray, "I keep my eyes always on the LORD . . . I will not be shaken" (Psalm 16:8).

If we're honest, we all struggle with these, probably on a daily basis. But no matter how we feel, the reality is that we *are* resilient enough and disciplined enough to keep our emotions in check. We will not be able to control how we feel at all times, but we *can* control our actions and how we treat others, even in the midst of those powerful feelings.

Emotional tendencies like jealousy, irritability, and distrust are a poison that can spread and impact every area of our lives if we are not careful. Have you ever had the experience of getting angry or frustrated and then your emotions just spiral out of control, spreading onto anyone and anything that comes your way? This kind of uncontrolled emotional release creates unnecessary tension or strain on our relationships, and it can often be hard to work our way out of the mess we've created. Here are a few ways to practice keeping our responses to these emotions in check:

- **Delay your reaction.** Have you ever said something in haste only to regret it later? Instead take a deep breath, count to ten, assess the situation, and try to remain calm, distancing your emotions from the incident or situation.
- **Find a healthy outlet for your frustrations and irritations**. Is there someone you can confide in? Is there a verse you can memorize and say to yourself often? Is there a prayer you can whisper? Is there a song you can sing that will quiet you?
- **See the emotion for what it is**. Too often we lash out or react quickly by getting sucked into the moment and thinking this is "always" the way it's going to be. Your life is bigger than what's right in front of you. This feeling will pass.
- **Ask God to give you peace**. Ask for divine help in the moment of high emotion and keep in mind that everything that happens to us in life can help us to become more like Christ. It may seem cliché, but God really can grant you the grace you need to handle the stressors that come your way, if you'll only ask for God's help.

Day 19

"Am I honest in all my actions and words, or do I exaggerate?"

When I was a kid, my family moved around a lot while my dad served in the US Navy. We moved often enough that I felt like I was always scrambling to make new friends, so part of the way I'd cope was to make up stories about my past every time I got to a new place. I wanted people to like me, so I would make up stories or exaggerate the facts in order to make people think I was interesting enough to be friends with. One time I vividly remember telling my friends that my older brother had a fiery red Corvette and that when I was older he was going to give it to me to drive. So when my friends met my brother for the first time and watched him climb out of a rusty old pickup truck, one of my friends asked, "Where is your Corvette?" "Corvette!" my brother replied. "Ha! I wish." Ouch. I was outed.

I think Wesley meant this question to do three things. First, his question asks us to consider how content we are in our lives. Are we content, or do we always want more? Contentment comes from a spirit of gratitude, and God desires that we are grateful people who learn to make the most of what we have.

Second, this question challenges us to be true to our identity in Christ, not to our identity in self. When we find our identity in Christ, we recognize that we are valued as a person regardless of our successes or failures, our possessions or poverty, or what we can do for God. Christ loves us for who we are as a child of God, not for what we do or what we have. Finally, I believe Wesley wants us to reflect on our character. We are, after all, made in the image of God. We've been created to reflect the love of God to everyone we come into contact with, and we cannot do that when we lie or are dishonest.

Let's face it—sometimes we lie. Sometimes we exaggerate. Sometimes we pretend we are

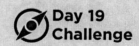

Day 19 Challenge

Read Colossians 3:9. Commit to a "no exaggeration, no lie" policy for the next twenty-four hours. Resist the urge to blame a "traffic jam" on your lateness or to blame your sibling for losing something you misplaced.

more important than we really are. We want to be liked, so we add on or take away from the truth so that we are seen in a more positive light. It happens to all of us at some time or another. Be encouraged! God is a God of second chances. Throughout the Bible we read numerous stories of people who have deceived God or others and who God has forgiven and welcomed with open arms. So don't waste your time running around, trying to keep your lie or exaggeration afloat. Instead, confess your offense and live in freedom from the guilt and shame.

Day 20

"Is there anyone I fear, dislike, disown, criticize, hold resentment toward, or disregard?"

Day 20 Challenge

Take a minute to talk with a person whom you typically try to avoid. How can you show this person the love of Christ today?

Today's question covers a lot of ground and gives us a lot to consider. But at the heart of the question is, Am I following Jesus' commands to love other people, even those who don't look like me or act like me or who are even hard to get along with? This is an important question to consider, because the negative way we feel toward people who are different from us can often create separation and tension in our lives and in our communities.

We typically feel fear, dislike, or resent others for many reasons. Maybe we assume we are better than they are. Maybe we just don't like his or her personality. Maybe someone has hurt us, and so we're done with that person altogether. Those are all typical human responses, but if we look to Jesus, we see a different way to respond.

Read Mark 10:46-52, a story about Jesus' encounter with a blind beggar, who was definitely an outsider in his community. In this encounter, we see how Jesus demonstrates a love for *all* people in *all* situations and circumstances, and he models for us how to demonstrate this love. Regardless of how hard it may be, a challenge in the Christian life is to be like Christ, and that means valuing and loving all people, as he showed us how to do. Sometimes this comes easy, and sometimes it means that we must work to see people as God sees them—as beloved children, of great value and worth.

Once I was working with a team of people on a project and one of the key leaders came to me and said, "I can't do this anymore. ['So and So'] is driving me crazy!" About an hour later "So and So" came to me and said, "['What's His Name'] is totally annoying." I kid you not—the two people were talking about each other! So just remember, for every person who "drives you crazy" there is most likely a person who you "drive crazy" too. We are not going to be totally compatible with everyone, it is true, but are we called to be people who are compatible, or people who are compassionate? Compassion for others is what Jesus modeled for us, again and again.

Day 21
"When did I last speak to someone about my faith?"

In Jesus' parting instructions to his disciples, he said, "I've received all authority in heaven and on earth. Therefore, go and make disciples of all nations, baptizing them in the name of the Father and of the Son and of the Holy Spirit, teaching them to obey everything that I've commanded you. Look, I myself will be with you every day until the end of this present age." (Matthew 28:19-20 CEB). When Wesley challenges us with the question, "When did I last speak to someone about my faith?" he is directly encouraging us to take up the challenge Jesus gave to his disciples to tell his story to the world. When we share our faith through our words and our actions, we fulfill the challenge that Jesus gave the disciples and the church to (1) go, (2) obey, and (3) listen to the Holy Spirit.

To "go" is to live on mission, to tell the story about what God has done and is doing today. To make sharing the gospel with your family, friends, and those around you a way of life. To "obey" is to live as Jesus models for us to live. Jesus came not only to die for us but also to show us how to live—as people who bear the image of a loving and holy God. To "obey" is to live holy lives characterized by love. When we live for God and others, we obey as Jesus challenged us to do.

To "listen to the Holy Spirit" means we look to God for direction. God's will is that the world be made whole, and we believers are meant to participate with God's mission to restore the world. The Holy Spirit

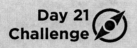

Day 21 Challenge

Actively look for ways to share your faith through your words, actions, or both today. Ask God to direct you to people or situations where you can be God's hands and feet in the world.

gives us strength, courage, and direction to make decisions that align us with God's mission. The Holy Spirit, our companion for the journey that is life, comforts, teaches, and reminds us to live a life of obedience to God.

To respond faithfully to Wesley's question "When did I last speak about my faith?" is to live a life of going, obeying, and listening to the Holy Spirit, realizing that each one of us is sent into the world to be the hands and feet of Jesus. We proclaim the gospel with our words, and we put the gospel into action through acts of mercy, compassion, and social justice. When we take time to serve those who are in need, whether with food, shelter, love, or safety, and do it in the name of the Father, the Son, and the Holy Spirit, we perform the gospel and remind people that we haven't forgotten them, and God has not forgotten them either.

Going Deeper

Take a quick look at the news headlines any given day of the week, and you'll read, in vivid detail, about all of the ways we human beings fail each other. Too often we are guilty of self-protection, for looking out for ourselves above anyone else. We live out of our own insecurities, which cause us to compare, disregard, and dismiss others as valued children of God. But Jesus models for us a different way to live. Throughout the Gospels, Jesus shows compassion to those whom society has pushed away. He remembers the forgotten. He reacts with love when others show him disrespect and hatred. He corrects and responds lovingly when he sees that people are hurting. He points them toward the Father.

Jesus could do all these things because he was allowing God's strength and love to flow through him. He was able to be on mission with what God wanted to do in the world. And that is the only way we can follow what Jesus modeled—to rely on God's perfect strength and love and then give them to the world. Jesus said,

> Therefore, my loved ones, just as you always obey me, not just when I am present but now even more while I am away, carry out your own salvation with fear and trembling. God is the one who enables you both to want and to actually live out his good purposes. Do everything without grumbling and arguing so that you may be blameless and pure, innocent children of God surrounded by people who are crooked and corrupt. Among these people you shine like stars in the world because you hold on to the word of life.
>
> Philippians 2:12-16 CEB

Isn't that encouraging? So often we beat ourselves up for all the ways we fall short, but Jesus says we don't have to do it on our own. He says, "God is the one who enables you both to want and to actually live out his good purposes" (v. 13). God is the one who gives us both the desire *and* the ability to love others as we are called to do, preparing and equipping our hearts to join Jesus in his mission to spread God's love throughout the world.

How can you draw from the vast depths of God's strength to follow Jesus and to respond the way he responded to others? How does embracing God's love and acceptance of you allow you to offer that same love and acceptance to others?

Sharing Thoughts and Feelings

Spend some time with a group discussing these questions.

- In what ways are you tempted to compare yourself to others? How do you think that affects your view of others and relationships with them?
- In what environments, or with what groups of people, do you feel most like yourself? Do you find that you "fake it" in certain situations? If so, why do you think you do that?
- What does it mean to have trust in a relationship? What qualities do you value in your friendships?

59

- In Wesley's question, "Am I jealous, impure, critical, irritable, touchy, or distrustful?" which of these descriptions do you struggle most with? Why do you think that is, or how have you felt the Lord speaking to you about this quality?
- How did Jesus respond to those people who were on the "outside"? With what groups of people do you feel the most unity? When you encounter someone who is different from you, how do you typically respond?
- Who first shared their faith with you? Do you tend to show your faith more through your words or deeds? Is there anyone the Lord is leading you to share your faith with right now?
- How have the last twenty-one days encouraged you in your practice of drawing nearer to the Lord? What is the Lord teaching you about the changes you can make in your life to join in God's mission for the world?

Doing Things Together

Truth or Lies?
Supplies needed: Pen or pencil and paper for each participant

Sometimes it's easy to tell when someone's "faking it," and other times it's not so easy. How good are you at "faking it"?

On a piece of paper, have each person write down three facts about themselves. Two of the statements should be true, and one should be false. (If this is done within a group of people who know one another well, try to make the true statements little-known facts about you, ones that are not obvious or well-known within the group.)

Have each person read his or her three statements, and have the group try to guess which statements are true, and which one of the statements is the lie. After all guesses have been made, the person can reveal the truths and the lie.

Discuss:

- Is it always easy to tell when someone is faking the truth about who he or she is?
- Are there certain environments in your life where you feel like you have to "fake it"? (It may be in church!) Why do you think you feel that way?

- How does knowing that you have a secure, permanent position as a child of God challenge your need to "fake it" in your life?

Knowing Our Place
Supplies needed: one or two decks of playing cards, a Bible

Divide a deck of playing cards into face cards (Jack, Queen, King) and low number cards (such as numbers 2 to 5). You will need one card for each participant. (If possible, try to have enough cards so that you can divide the group as evenly as possible—for instance, if you have ten people, try to have five face cards and five low-number cards available. If your group is large, you might need to pull from more than one deck of cards.)

Shuffle the cards face down, and give each person one card. Tell them not to look at their cards, but know that face cards are more important than low-number cards. When you say go, have each person put the card face-out on his or her forehead so that it is visible to others. Then have participants walk around the room, interacting with one another for a minute or two—but without telling other people what cards they have.

Then—still not looking at your own cards!—tell people to gather with the people they think have the same cards as they do (that is, face cards with face cards; low cards with low cards). Now tell everyone to look at their cards.

Discuss:

- Why did you join the group you did? What made you think you had a face card or a low card?
- If you had a face card, how did others treat you? How did it make you feel?
- If you had a low card, how did others treat you? How did it make you feel?
- What can this exercise tell us about how we tend to treat other people, and what value we assign to them?
- Read Mark 10:46-52, a story about Jesus' encounter with a blind beggar, an outsider in his community. How does Jesus respond to this man, who had definitely been dealt a "low number" card? What can Jesus' response teach us?

Listening for God

God, thank you for the opportunity to walk with you throughout my life. Thank you for never leaving me and for giving me everything I need to live in partnership with you on your mission for this world. Help me to embrace the love and grace you have so graciously given me and to give that same love and grace away to others, in your name. Thank you for loving me and giving me a place at your table, as your precious child. In Jesus' name. Amen.

Notes and Thoughts for Week 3

CPSIA information can be obtained
at www.ICGtesting.com
Printed in the USA
LVOW10s0413301017
553924LV00009B/9/P